Preface

As a young girl, I lost my voice to circumstances in my life.

As I have grown in Christ my voice has returned, never to

go quiet or silent again. The Lord poured these

words out of me so I could pour into you.

Be blessed.

The voice of the Lord is over the waters; The God of glory thunders; The Lord is over many waters. The voice of the Lord is powerful; The voice of the Lord is full of majesty.

Psalms 29:3-4 NKJV

Voice

You called me to use my voice and with a choice my voice

is activated, telling of a love for me in a time so sweet.

A voice You expanded to be used equivalently. With my

voice I go on and on; learning how to pick up Your still small voice

that will tell me no wrong.

My Voice

My voice will be confident

My voice will be bold

My voice will be loud

My voice will speak righteousness

My voice will speak for justice

My voice will be soft

My voice will be authoritative

My voice will laugh

My voice will smile

My voice will love

My voice

Be Used

Do not sit quietly, the world is waiting to hear a voice so captivating. Speaking truth and justice bound, freeing those whose life is not sound. Tell it, tell it everywhere, someone is listening who is in despair. It is okay to be used by the one who lit your fuse. Your fuse was lit for others to see, it is okay just to be me.

Speak

You speak to me, you speak through me

You speak

You speak at me, you speak over me

You speak

You speak ownership, you speak creation

You speak

You speak oneness, you speak fellowship

You speak

You speak wholeness, you speak deliverance

You speak

You speak grace, you speak mercy

You speak

You speak love, unconditional love, it is what

You speak

Praise

I use my voice to praise in every way, no matter the

pitch, tone, or day. My mouth is an instrument designed

to give praise. I open it up for Your glory to be raised.

I praise in good; I praise in bad; I will continue to

praise with all I have. I use my voice to praise in every

way no matter the pitch, tone, or day.

Gentle

An angry giant can be soothed with a gentle voice,

their fire squashed and their stance brought low. Gentle

words continue to flow as it brings the giant to be no more. Keep

it soft and continue on, do not build it up, you have weathered

the storm. Gentle, gentle, gentle you go, the angry giant is

no more.

Use It

You told me to use my voice with boldness and

without fear. Do not hold back from Your truth, but speak truth with

love. Do not go for the half-truth, it is not a part of you. I should not hide Your

truth just to be nice, I hide You in the process, for you are

my shining light.

Receive It

Spoken in truth and in love, open your heart to the message

from above. No confusion or irritation speaking the

truth, it is part of the equation. Take it in, as it is for my

good, no matter how hard the acceptance is. Getting it

right all the time is not a completed task. But receiving the truth

removes the mask. Receive it in love, receive it

in truth, it is the best thing we could ever do.

From Within

When I speak from within there is no end. The flow

is ever gushing until I am empty again. Truth

be told and story to unfold from within centered around You.

I let go of me, so it is not I who speaks to hear myself

talking, struggling to connect. As I go from within, time

and time again the connection is there and I do not talk in despair,

because I speak from within.

Your Voice

Your voice is comfort.

Your voice is a warm blanket.

Your voice is a loving hug.

Your voice is a promise.

Your voice is a devoted spouse.

Your voice is unending.

Your voice is my rest.

Your voice is my awakening.

Your voice is love.

Guidance

I hear Your voice today, You had my
voice silent as You led the way.
Your voice spoke guidance; Your
voice spoke compassion and surety.
Your voice guides me to every blessing.

Understand

Your voice allows me to understand Your word of life as I read and study it.

Your voice gives image to Your word and helps me to understand. Your voice teaches me Your word to a degree of understanding why

Your voice is a voice of understanding.

Knowing When

Silence is a voice at times, it is the listening voice

that often should have the volume on high.

Knowing when to tune in and to shut out any other.

Benefits are exposed in knowing when to have the quiet

of quiet with a focus to hear and the knowing when.

Words

The words we speak is our voice

They can show love or hate.

Words of love encourage, energize, and

are pleasant; words of hate criticize, complain, and are

untrue. Remember the words we sow, we shall also

reap.

Justice

Speak out for justice with boldness, it pushes the unjust out of the way. Justice is for all, as all voices can speak it, as it keeps fear in its place. Do not let injustice pass, use your voice and put it on blast.

Apology

My voice asked for forgiveness, acknowledging

the offense with sound from my actions.

Humbling my heart as the words "please forgive me"

are spoken out loud. Seeking closure to a wrong by

doing what is right with my voice.

Please accept my apology.

Voice of Freedom

I rejoice at being free, as my soul and mind have been set free. I will continue to walk in freedom because I have no space for anything unworthy. For I voice love, kindness, justice, patience, and meekness, all of what my Spirit connects to and lives on. The Spirit of freedom lives in me and I rejoice for being free.

Now I Know

My voice is a tool to be used for good. I will use it with boldness and confidence.

I will speak what is good and no one on Earth can stop it because I speak from within.

Now I know how to use my voice, to bind in love; to pull

together; and to add to; to loose; to cast down; and to get rid of.

I will not forget, because now I know.

Healing Balm

My voice can be a balm to soothe the mind, heart, and soul. My voice can heal many wounds as it was called to do. Do not shut it down, many are in need to have a balm to comfort and heal their needs.

Song

Sing from your soul the song
of your heart. Sing it out
loud, even in part. Please
no one else but the Creator of
sound. Sing His words and
make Him proud.

A Powerful Tool

So many different facets to the sound, and how it is projected while others are around. Excitement, zest, authority, and projection are good to use, for what you have been given from Love.

I Speak

I speak life over everything dear and I

speak life more abundantly to you my beloved.

I speak healing to your mind, body, and soul, as I speak an

overabundance of more than you can hold.

I speak encouragement to your inner being, not

knowing the road where you are heading.

I speak love to let you know, I am near and that I

never left you, for I know what you can bear.

Talk to Me

Come sit, and tell me what is on your mind. Talk

to Me, I have the time. Come relax and bend

My ear. Your voice is the sound I love to hear.

Again, talk to Me, I have the time. It is your

choice, but remember you have always been

Mine.

Over Yourself

It no one else does it, it is okay

to speak over yourself.

If you have not heard it, it is okay

to speak over yourself.

Do not doubt it, it is okay

to speak over yourself.

Reject It

Let your voice be loud and clear

to reject all negative in your ear.

Let your voice renounce every word

known and unknown and curses heard.

Reject it of old; reject it of new; and reject all

of what is not good for you.

For Us

This tool we have is for us. The most important responsibility of this tool is to speak up. To sow words of encouragement, truth, and love as it is designed to work in excellence.

It is for us to use this tool to benefit others, but most importantly it is for us to use this tool with others in mind.

Found It!

You found it!

Do not stop using it.

You found it!

Put it to good use.

You found it!

Do no harm.

You found it!

Let justice sound out.

You found it!

Expose

Expose what is true

Expose what is you

Expose what is pure

Expose what is a cure

Expose what is false

and replace it with your pulse.

Myself

What I speak over myself should uplift, encourage, and take action. What I speak over myself will activate what is within. What I speak over myself will give me life.

Who Does Not Love, Loved Me Never

Do you love Me, yes I do.

Do you love Me, yes I do.

Do you love Me, you know I do.

Do you love Me, yes I do.

Do you love Me, yes I do.

Do you love Me, you know I do.

Push Back

As my voice comes out it will push back,

on what is not of You. As my voice makes sound it

will push back to make sure the sound carries.

So push back.

Naturally Good

Given to me, so it is naturally good.

Given to be used, so it is naturally good.

Given to be heard, so it is naturally good.

To Stop It

STOP! I said STOP!

Never again will I stand for it.

My voice is to stop it, to end the cycle.

To stop it and take its life.

STOP!

To Teach

As my voice leads by example, it will teach other voices to be strong, confident, mighty, brave, and bold. To teach is to lead by example, to project with strength, assurance, power, fearlessness, and daring candor. To teach is to be transparent.

Talk Up

What will you say, how will it come out?
You have to talk up. How will they know or
show it where to go? You have to talk up.
Say the words, you know its name and put
it to shame, you have to talk up.

Tell The Story

Voice the beginning; recount the middle; and give the proper ending of telling the story. The voice of every story is different and needs to be heard. Each story brings freedom and light. So tell the story and let it take flight.

You Never Know

You never know who is listening.

You never know who you are helping.

You never know who will pass it on.

You never know who else needs to

Sound the alarm.

Do Not Be Afraid

Do not be afraid to release your voice. It was given to you for a purpose. Do not be afraid to say something, your voice was given to you for a purpose. Do not be afraid to release your voice, the life you save may be your very own.

Be Pleasant

A pleasant voice carries a lot of weight.

A pleasant voice births a pleasant smile.

A pleasant voice builds a strong foundation

for pleasant words.

Don't Hold Back

Don't hold your voice back, let it go!

Don't hold your voice back, let it flow.

Don't hold your voice back, it is a part of your glow.

Don't hold your voice back, you never know

who it captivates when they see it is not a show.

From the Inside Out

What you bring forth always starts from the inside out. What you hear from within always comes upward and out. Rejoice in being led to speak from the inside out. It is indeed a good guide in using your inside voice.

Awesome

Your voice is awesome.

Awesome is your voice.

Your sound is awesome.

Awesome is your sound.

Your voice is unique.

Awesome is your unique voice.

Let awesome ring out in your voice.

Awesome is your voice to ring out.

Your words are awesome.

Awesome are your words.

In Every Season

Let your voice ring out in every season.

Spring, summer, winter, and fall,

use your voice through it all.

Happiness, sadness, in grief or despair,

use your voice to bring in prayer.

There is even a season to give your voice rest.

In every season, give your best.

Discovery

How magnificent it is to discover your sound.

You cannot go back to quietness now. You have

opened the door and awakened a jewel, given

to you specifically. What a perfect find of

something so grand, a discovery worth finding as

your sound echoes throughout the land.

As a Child

Learning how to use your voice was an everyday

lesson. Learning how to speak was not

something that happened overnight. Day by day; month by

month; and year by year your voice was being

born with sound to make words and

conversations, but most importantly to

communicate.

Not Voiceless

Even though there are those who are voiceless,

Nevertheless, you are not voiceless.

Let your words be known through your hands

and in your writing. These tools are given so you

can have a voice and not be voiceless.

One Part of the Whole Body

There are many parts to our body and our voice is one of importance.

This sound can express how the whole body feels, this sound can speak over the whole body, and

this sound can protect the whole body. How useful is this one part of the whole body.

The Voice Effect

Your voice affects others by how it is used

towards them. If you want to make someone happy,

your voice will be cheerful. Lift up your voice to encourage others.

If you want to show you care, your voice will give

love and this is called the voice effect.

Open Vault

You know the combination to unlock the openness

of your voice. Simply start talking and never close it

up in a vault again. There is so much to gain with an

open door with open opportunities.

An open vault that opens to show what is valuable inside.

And your voice is valuable. Right, left, right, and hear the click.

Hostage

Your voice should not hold you hostage as it should not hold another person hostage. Just as another person should not hold your voice hostage.

Release and be set free; free the one who needs to be

set free; and speak out to be heard.

Respectfully

Your voice will allow you to respectfully disagree and

still love. Respectfully agree and voice gladness.

This character trait of your voice goes a long way.

Ask

If you do not understand, use your voice and ask.

Use your voice to seek an answer to the wonder

of your mind. There is no wrong question, and

it is always good to ask.

Knows

If your heart and mind know truth,

the voice will follow suit. Your

voice will end the run of a lie with

truth. Your voice knows truth is light and life.

You Can Tell

Your voice is your defense against anything

unpleasant that should not be. So yes, you can tell.

Use your voice to put it out there to stop what is

unpleasant. Go ahead, you can tell.

Cannot Take It Back

My voice will need to be careful in what

is said, my mouth cannot take it back. My voice should

not speak hastily, my mouth cannot take it back. My

voice should take a moment before responding, so

my mouth will not have to find a way to take it back.

Calling

If you say it, your voice is calling you to it.

If you say it, then by all means

answer your calling. If you say it,

the reality of your calling comes true.

Allow

Allow creations to flow out of your voice.

Allow your voice to set the atmosphere.

Allow your voice to control your choice

and allow your voice to speak truth.

Take Down

Your voice can take down the giant. Have no fear, your voice takes its rightful authority, as it takes down all fear and anxiety approaching you. So use your authority and let your voice take down all that is not love.

What You See

What do you see? Give voice to it, describe the beauty of what you see. As there is beauty in what you see, speak a good word in the direction of what you see. So, what do You see?

I Give

I give my voice to goodness.

I give my voice to praise.

I give my voice to singing, but I

do not give my voice to shame.

I give my voice to power.

I give my voice to strength.

I give my voice to endurance, but

I do not give my voice to fits.

I give.

No Rest

There will be a time when your voice will need rest.

Do not let it go for periods of time with no rest,

it is not healthy. You will know when to give it rest.

Your voice is important, as is rest.

Take it.

Cry Out

I will cry out in joy.

I will cry out in sadness.

I will cry out in celebration and

I will cry out in pain.

I will cry out for help.

I will cry out in victory.

The point is that I will cry out.

How Long

How long has your voice been silent?

How long has it not voiced a sound; an

opinion; encouraged; told a truth; and expressed

a feeling or thought? The truth is it does not

matter how long it's been. You can start now.

If I

If I do not use my voice, it will not be heard.

If I do not voice my feelings, then I stay trapped.

If I do not voice love, I cannot heal.

If I use my voice to encourage love, I see love.

If I use my voice to uplift, I feel uplifted.

If I use my voice, I will be heard.

What I Speak

What I speak over me matters.

The words that come forth have consequences.

What I speak over me matters.

It is a life worth living.

What I speak over me matters.

How I feel from the inside out is a product of what I speak over me.

www.ingramcontent.com/pod-product-compliance
Lightning Source LLC
Chambersburg PA
CBHW061343040426
42444CB00011B/3055